Stress Less

Tips and Tools to Help You CHILL

Helaine Becker

Scholastic Canada Ltd.

Toronto New York London Auckland Sydney
Mexico City New Delhi Hong Kong Buenos Aires

Scholastic Canada Ltd.
604 King Street West, Toronto, Ontario M5V IEI, Canada

Scholastic Inc.
557 Broadway, New York, NY 10012, USA

Scholastic Australia Pty Limited
PO Box 579, Gosford, NSW 2250, Australia

Scholastic New Zealand Limited
Private Bag 94407, Botany, Manukau 2163, New Zealand

Scholastic Children's Books
Euston House, 24 Eversholt Street, London NWI IDB, UK

www.scholastic.ca

Library and Archives Canada Cataloguing in Publication

Becker, Helaine, 1961-, author
Stress less : tips and tools to help you chill / Helaine Becker.

ISBN 978-1-4431-4870-2 (softcover)

1. Stress management for children--Juvenile literature.
2. Stress in children--Juvenile literature. 3. Stress (Psychology)--
Juvenile literature. I. Title.

BF723.S75B45 2018   j155.4'189042   C2017-906436-3

Photo credits: Photos ©: cover background, back cover: INDECcraft/iStockphoto; cover
popsicles: smartboy10/iStockphoto; 1: smartboy10/iStockphoto; 3 comet and throughout:
vectortatu/iStockphoto; 6: Shanina/iStockphoto; 7 star and throughout: ulimi/iStockphoto;
8-9: Marina Lazinina/iStockphoto; 11: bobotr/iStockphoto; 13: kolb_art/iStockphoto; 14
bottom: Drawkman/iStockphoto; 16-17: blindspot/iStockphoto; 18: yayayoyo/iStockphoto;
20-21 background: Dreaming_Lucy/iStockphoto; 22-23 background: befehr/iStockphoto;
24 bottom: BoxerX/iStockphoto; 26 right: eduardrobert/iStockphoto; 28-29 background:
royyimzy/iStockphoto; 30-31 background: tigerstrawberry/iStockphoto; 32-33: RamCreativ/
iStockphoto; 35 bottom: appleuzr/iStockphoto; 37: mingcreative/iStockphoto; 39: Thoth_
Adan/iStockphoto; 40: cteconsulting/iStockphoto; 42: Shanina/iStockphoto; 44-45: jjaakk/
iStockphoto; 46-47: thanaphiphat/iStockphoto; 48-49 background: Lesikvit/iStockphoto; 50-51:
excape25/iStockphoto; 52-53 smiley faces: calvindexter/iStockphoto; 54-55: Svetlana Aganina/
iStockphoto; 56-57: ScottTalent/iStockphoto; 58-59 background: IAtelier/iStockphoto; 58
bottom: Bullet_Chained/iStockphoto; 60-61 food icons: venimo/iStockphoto; 62-63: lushik/
iStockphoto; 64-65: saemilee/iStockphoto; 66-67: bagira22/iStockphoto; 68-69: Piyanat
Nethaisong/iStockphoto; 70-71: Serhii Brovko/iStockphoto; 72-73: CurvaBezier/iStockphoto; 74:
Irina_Qiwi/iStockphoto; 77: blocberry/Shutterstock; 78: CandO_Designs/iStockphoto; 80-81
background: dariooo/iStockphoto; 82-83: Diane Labombarbe/iStockphoto; 84-85 background:
A-Digit/iStockphoto; 86-87 background: tronand/iStockphoto; 88: FrankRamspott/
iStockphoto; 90-91 background: JoeLena/iStockphoto; 92-93: iLexx/iStockphoto; 95: Ylivdesign/
iStockphoto; 96: Ani_Ka/iStockphoto.

6 5 4 3 2 1   Printed in Canada 121   18 19 20 21 22

MIX
Paper from
responsible sources
FSC® C004071

Table of Contents

Introduction

The secret is out: kids' lives can be challenging. Homework, piano lessons, soccer practice, household chores (Did you make your bed?), packing your lunch (Don't forget the apple!), flossing.

Plus you've got a whole world of people that you deal with every day — family, friends, frenemies, the kid down the block, your teacher . . .

It takes so much energy! No wonder you sometimes feel like it's all too much.

This book, and its companion title, *Don't Stress: How to Handle Life's Little Problems*, is meant to help make life's stresses more manageable. It's full of tips and strategies to help you keep your cool when you feel hot under the collar. It offers practical advice on how to tackle tricky situations and reinforce your ability to handle challenges with grace.

So get comfy (page 32), take a deep breath (page 41) and start reading (page 88). You'll be glad you did!

Be Yourself

There's no one like you. You bring to the world a unique set of talents, quirks and viewpoints. You can stress yourself out trying to be like someone else, or like a fantasy you that's taller, smarter, more popular. Or you can be yourself and reap the rewards that come from being true to you.

Your skin fits you perfectly. Own it.

If plan A doesn't work, remember that the alphabet has 25 more letters.

It's Not Just You

When things go wrong, and you feel frustrated and overwhelmed, you might think things will *never* go your way — that the universe is out to get you and things like this don't happen to other people.

Not true. Things don't just go wrong for you. The world is imperfect. People make mistakes. Software has bugs. Time runs out.

Feeling frustrated on occasion is completely normal. It can even be helpful because frustration drives you to make changes that will help you solve your problems in the long-run. So take a breath. Take a break. Then come back and take another crack at it.

Twiddle Your Thumbs

Keeping your hands moving is one way to help your mind stay calmer and more focused. Twiddling your thumbs is an easy way to do that. Just clasp your hands together and rotate your thumbs around each other. Then try it in the other direction.

Play with Some Beads

Toys for fidgety fingers have been popular worldwide for eons. That's because doing repetitive motions with your hands, like knitting, typing or playing with worry beads, soothes the mind and body. It interferes with the part of your brain that processes distressing situations. Busy hands mean a calmer brain.

In Greece and Cyprus, for example, people play with worry beads when they've got something on their minds, or when they're feeling restless. These strands of beads feel nice in your hand and they make a satisfying *chunk-chunk-chunk* sound when they slide into each other. They can be funky-looking too!

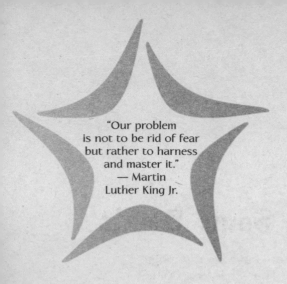

"Our problem
is not to be rid of fear
but rather to harness
and master it."
— Martin
Luther King Jr.

Face Your Fears

Everyone is afraid of something. Some fears won't make much difference to your life — if you live in the mountains and you're afraid of sharks, you shouldn't have a problem. But what if you're afraid of something that *can* hold you back, like public speaking?

There's only one way forward: face your fears.

If speaking in front of a crowd sends you snaky, confront your fear by taking on small, manageable challenges, like giving a short talk in front of your family. Gradually take on more challenges, like making a presentation to your class, then your whole grade. It might sound crazy-scary, but this technique really works. By facing your fears, you shrink them down in size. You take away their power to control you. Instead, you control them.

Chew Sugar-Free Gum

Chomp, chomp, chomp — chewing gum can actually be good for you. It can help reduce levels of the stress hormone cortisol. Choose sugarless gum to protect your teeth, and you've got a winning way to cut stress down to size.

11

> "Strength does not come from physical capacity. It comes from an indomitable will."
> — Mohandas Gandhi

Stand Your Ground

Most people don't enjoy confrontation. Putting yourself out there just feels too scary. But when you don't stand up for yourself it feels terrible. You might even feel powerless, which adds stress.

When you take control of a situation, you gain pride and confidence.

Some great ways to stand your ground:

- If someone is pressing you to do something you don't want to do, say: "That doesn't work for me." Repeat as necessary.

- Speak in a loud, clear, firm voice and make eye contact with your adversary as you state your position.

- If someone insults you, resist the urge to get drawn in and insult them back. Use calm, clear, respectful language.

- Call it like you see it. If something isn't fair, or if someone is being a bully, say so: "Friends don't treat friends like that." "That wasn't funny; it was mean." "Not cool."

Try a Martial Art

Any of the martial arts — such as karate, judo, jiu-jitsu, tae kwon do or tai chi — are terrific for building focus and busting stress. Tai chi's slow movements are ideal for inducing relaxation. More vigorous martial arts, like judo or jiu-jitsu, let you work up a sweat while you dial down the nervous energy.

All of the martial arts help build your confidence. When you spar with a partner or perform a *kata* in front of your instructor, you learn to control your emotions and conquer your fears.

Best of all, martial arts are a real kick.

Look at Pictures of Cats

Or puppies or bunnies or any other cute critter that makes you go "*Awwww*."

Cutesy pictures make you feel good. But they do something else too. According to a recent study, people who looked at images of cute animals or cartoony characters performed better on tasks that required focus afterward. They also showed better results on tasks that required manual dexterity.

It's Easy as 1-2-3

Do you sometimes get distracted when you're supposed to be completing a task? You're not the only one! Follow this simple three-step process to help you stay on track and get the job done.

1. Get in gear. Get yourself to the right place, at the right time. Bring the stuff you need to complete the task.

2. Get on it. Put your head down and get started — no ifs, ands or buts.

3. Get it right. Once you've finished the task, check your work and put on the finishing touches, which might be adding your name to the top of your homework or stowing it neatly in your backpack so you don't forget to take it to school.

Listen to Your Heartbeat

Put your hand over your heart. Can you feel its beat through your fingers?

Your heart is a musical instrument that you already know how to play.

If you're feeling out of sorts or overwhelmed, the sound and feel of your heart acts as a powerful corrective. Close your eyes and really focus on the beat: *tha-thump, tha-thump, tha-thump.* If your heart is racing, consciously try to slow it down. The longer you listen, the calmer and more centred you'll feel.

Beat Stress by Drumming

Maybe you're the kind of kid who's always drumming on your desk, the table, your leg. Or maybe you've never touched a drum. Either way, drumming is a great way to let off steam.

Drumming keeps your hands busy, which lets your mind calm down and gives you something fun to focus on. And mastering a tricky rhythm can also give you a powerful sense of accomplishment.

Almost anything can serve as a drum — a plastic pail turned over, a box grater, a steel can. And anything can be a drumstick — a fork, a pencil, the palm of your hand.

There's no right or wrong. Play along to your favourite song or to the silent song in your soul.

Eye Spy with My Little Eye

When you're tired, your eyes get tired as well. Too much time looking at screens can also strain your eyes.

Give your eyes a break with this mini workout. It's like a massage for your eyeballs!

1. Without moving your head, look as far to the left as you can. Then look far to your right.
2. Look up — all the way up. Then down, down, down.
3. Face straight ahead and move your eyes in a circle three times. Repeat, moving them in the opposite direction.
4. Move your eyes in a figure eight, twice. Then again in the opposite direction.
5. Look at the bridge of your nose. Then the tip of your nose.
6. Close your eyes and roll them up and back. Then let your eyeballs relax and sink back into their sockets.

Declutter

Drawers that won't close, backpacks overflowing with old homework assignments, toy boxes full of nothing but old junk — all of these are irritations that can derail your day.

Streamline your space by getting rid of stuff you no longer need or want. Your gently used clothes or old toys can be passed along to a friend or family member, or given to charity. You'll reduce your daily dose of stress-inducing irritation, and benefit from the peace of mind that comes from being in a serene, visually soothing space. You'll also get the good feeling that comes from sharing with others.

"Tidy space, tidy mind."

Tag It

When your stuff is all organized and easy to find, you save yourself tons of time and frustration. But getting organized is one thing, and *staying* organized is another. To help with that task, try labelling each object's "home." You can use a label-maker or make your own tags with sticky notes, stickers or brightly coloured tape.

The name tags will help you remember where each object goes and remind you to put things away when you're finished with them. Using your new system, you'll become more efficient and able to find what you need faster. You'll be less stressed and have more time for fun!

Keep a Calendar

Your best pal's birthday was yesterday and you missed it. Even worse, you forgot that yesterday was the big spelling test and you didn't study. Now you're worried you lost a friend and got a bad grade. Talk about stress!

There's an easy way to keep those date-driven stress bombs from exploding. Use a calendar to keep track of dates, birthdays, homework due dates and events. A large wall calendar or in-your-face desktop version helps keep important dates in clear view.

Calendar quick-tips:

- Mark off important dates by outlining them in red marker.
- Highlight events with fun stickers so they're easy to see at a glance.
- Check your calendar daily.

Tongue twisters stretch your muscles *and* make you laugh. Try saying this five times fast: Rubber baby buggy bumpers

Stick Out Your Tongue

Your tongue is one of the most important organs in your body. It's made up of eight separate muscles that work together to give it strength and flexibility.

This mini workout for your tongue helps these muscles relax. And when they relax, you feel more relaxed too.

1. Moving in a clockwise direction, use the tip of your tongue to massage the inside of your mouth. Then repeat in the opposite direction.
2. Fold your tongue back and press the tip against the roof of your mouth.
3. Stick your tongue out as far as it can go.
4. Bring your tongue back in, close your mouth and squeeze your tongue so it's folded in half.
5. Finish by letting your tongue flatten and widen. Let your jaw soften too.
6. Relax.

Gently Down the Stream

You can't stop thinking about it — that embarrassing mistake you made in class, the unkind comment you overheard, that worry over your test. Here's how to send that thought packing:

Picture a small boat docked at the side of a river. Take your thought and mentally put it on the boat. Then untie the boat and push it into the current. Watch the boat — and your pesky problem — drift downriver and disappear around a bend. Don't forget to wave bye-bye.

Make a Decision

White shirt or red? Apple or banana?
Sometimes even the smallest decisions can feel
overwhelming.

Yet research shows that when people stop
waffling and make a decision — any decision
— they feel better about themselves and their
situation. They feel calmer too.

That remains true even if the decision turns out
to be less than perfect.

Decision-making is a skill; you get better at it
with practice. And the more decisions you make,
the more in control you feel.

So make decision-making a habit. Start small,
with low-risk choices like the colour of your
socks or which fruit to pack in your lunch. Then
when you are faced with a bigger decision, it
won't feel so daunting.

Decision-Making Strategy

When making decisions, follow this simple strategy to ensure you're on the right track.

1. Define the problem. What are the options you're choosing from?

2. Brainstorm possible solutions. Get help from friends, family members or experts (like a teacher) if you need It.

3. Evaluate each idea. Figure out what the consequences might be if you follow this course of action.

4. Decide on a solution.

5. Do a gut-check. Take a moment to see how your body feels right after the decision is made. Do you feel lighter? Relieved? Happy? Then it's probably a good choice. If you feel anxious, sweaty or sick to your stomach, that's a clue to reconsider your decision.

6. Carry it out.

7. Reflect on it. Once you've acted on a decision, don't forget to take a look back and evaluate it. Did everything play out the way you'd predicted? Are you still happy with the decision? This step will help you fine-tune your decision-making ability and help you make even better choices in the future.

"You miss one hundred percent of the shots you don't take."
— Wayne Gretzky

Take It to the Hoop

You've got the ball. You decide to go for the layup. But halfway to the hoop, a defender steps in your path. Do you back off or go for it?

A big part of decision-making is committing to a course of action. If you quit halfway, it's like you never made the decision in the first place. So dodge that defender and follow through! You may just sink that basket and score big for the team — and yourself.

Abandon Ship

"It seemed like a good idea at the time . . ."

Last night you made a decision: at lunch today, you'd go sit with that group of kids in the drama club and ask if you can join. But now there's another kid sitting with them — the school bully! Should you carry on with your plan or back off?

There is one situation where you *might* want to go back on a decision: when the circumstances have changed. That's a signal that it's time to make a *new* decision, one that takes advantage of all the information now at your fingertips. You might carry on with your original plan, but then again, you may realize it's wiser to change your course of action.

Be Flexible

No one can plan for every outcome of a given situation.

Sometimes, you just have to go with the flow.

Keep a Gratitude Journal

The sun warm on your shoulders, a friend's smile, a hot bowl of pho when your tummy is grumbling — there's so much to be grateful for.

It turns out that people who actively look for things to be grateful for are happier than those who don't. It doesn't even seem to matter if you find anything, it's the act of searching for them that matters.

So start a journal in which you record at least one thing that you feel grateful for every day. It builds the habit of appreciation and helps change your own attitude to one of joyful expectation.

"Gratitude is happiness doubled by wonder."
— G. K. Chesterton

This technique works
especially well
when you can't
get to sleep
at night.

Jam the Circuits

There are times when your mind won't stop.
Round and round it goes, chewing over the
same old worries, playing back the same old
memories.

How do you turn off the mental replay button?
One trick is to jam the circuits. Give yourself a
mental word challenge that is fairly dull, but will
make your mind work.

- Make a list of all the words you can think of
  that start with the letter C or D.

- Start with the name of a country — like
  France — then think of a country that
  starts with the last letter of that country's
  name: E. Ethiopia! Now think of a country
  that starts with A, etc. You can try this with
  cities or animals too.

- Choose a category, like "fruit" or "animals."
  Start with A for apple, then B for banana,
  and continue through the alphabet.

When you force yourself to think about
something else, the new thoughts interfere with
the repeating ones. Your mind can finally quiet.

Make Up a Mantra

A mantra is a repeated word, phrase or sound that helps quiet your mind's chatter so you feel more peaceful inside. People have used them for thousands of years as meditation tools. When you focus on a mantra, repeating it over and over again, it stops other thoughts from filling your mind.

You can use just about anything as a mantra. One of the most commonly used is the simple sound "*Om.*" Or choose a nonsense sound that is fun to repeat (like *ram-a-lam*) or a phrase that calls up a pleasant, relaxing image (like "silvery sands").

Get Comfy with Discomfort

Imagine you're taking a hike up a huge hill.

When you start, you're full of energy and enthusiasm. The hill isn't too steep and you feel like you can climb to the top no problem. But then the climb gets tougher. The hill grows steep. You lose your footing and stumble. You want to quit — it's just too hard!

But if you stick with it, suddenly the peak comes into view, the path levels out and you get a new burst of energy. You can reach your goal.

Learning is just like climbing up a hill. The process is called the learning curve. At the start of the process, like when you're learning to play an instrument, it feels just like the beginning of that hike: you're full of enthusiasm and energy. But as you continue, the hill gets steeper. You feel discomfort. You want to quit.

This is the point when most people *do* quit. They can't handle the uncomfortable feelings at the steepest part of the learning curve.

But if you stick it out, you know what will happen — the path will level out. It will get easier to climb, and before you know it you will reach the top — and success.

So get comfy with discomfort and recognize it for what it is — a mile marker on the way to mastery.

Life Is a Team Sport

Sure, you're the centre of your own life — see the *I* at the heart of "life"? But life is a team sport. No one gets through it without a supportive crew. And there is no *I* in "team."

To be a good team player, you need to think less about yourself and more about others. You pass the ball so someone else can score the goal. Hang tough on defence so your offensive players can get a chance to shine. And you show up for practice, day in and day out, even during weeks when you're on the disabled list.

When you live your life as a team player, you reap great rewards — even if your squad finishes in the cellar. You've made friends who've got your back for the long haul. And with friends like that, how can you lose?

Choose Your Team Wisely

Take a good, hard look at the people around you. Are the members of your "team" trustworthy, reliable and kind? If not, they will wind up letting you down when you need them.

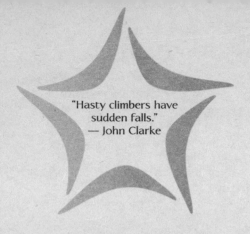

Haste Makes Waste

You're hurrying to get your breakfast because
you're late for school and you still haven't
packed your lunch. You yank open the fridge
and reach for the milk when — oh no! The eggs
crash to the floor and *SPLAT!* Now you have to
clean up the sticky, eggy mess, and you'll really
be late . . .

Have you ever noticed how things seem to go
wrong when you're in a hurry?

When you rush around like a chicken without
a head, you're bound to make mistakes. Tasks
can take even longer than they would if you
acted in a calmer manner, with slower and more
deliberate actions.

So when time is short, don't speed up — slow
down.

Slow It Down

With a million things on your plate, it's easy to get hyper. Your heart races, your mind races, you even talk a mile a minute.

When you feel yourself spinning into hyperspeed, take a moment to consciously slow your mind and body. Take a deep breath and hold it. Then let it out with a sigh.

Sit for a moment and close your eyes. Remind yourself that everything that can get done will get done. And if it doesn't, tomorrow is another day.

What Do You Hope to Achieve?

Your little sister has borrowed your favourite hoodie. Again. Without asking! Before you stomp into her room and lay into her, take some time to let your temper cool. Then ask yourself this one simple question: what do you hope to achieve?

Focusing on your end goal can help clarify your path. The action you are considering might be appealing (like telling off your kid sister for borrowing your sweater), but will it help achieve your goal (getting your sister to ask before she borrows something)? Probably not. She might wind up taking more stuff just to get back at you for blasting her.

Maybe a quiet conversation, during which you tell her you're happy to let her borrow your things, as long as she asks first, is really the route to take. You'll solve your problem, avoid a fight and reduce the amount of stress in your life.

The Eyes Have It

Go ahead — look 'em straight in the eye.

Direct eye contact can help stimulate the release of a hormone called oxytocin, which makes people feel warm and affectionate toward each other. So looking at someone directly and smiling is a natural way to make you both feel good.

Smell It!

Close your eyes and take a deep breath.
What do you smell?

Making a conscious effort to notice the scents
around you helps get you out of your head. It
helps you be present.

Follow Your Nose

Do you know that pleasant scents can help you relax? The smell of lavender, for example, is said to have soothing properties. It can also help promote sleep.

Any fragrance that appeals to you can be soothing. Some people enjoy the smell of lemons, others the scent of fresh-cut grass. Whichever you prefer, getting a whiff of a fragrance you like can help you feel happier and calmer.

Breathe

Need a breather? Then take one. Take a minute to focus on your breath.

Breathe in deeply through your nose. Feel your lungs fill from way down deep in your abdomen all the way up to your chest. Then let it out again with a sigh.

Repeat three or four times.

Doesn't that feel better?

Picture It

When you've had a tough day, use this simple visualization exercise to help put it behind you:

1. Lie down someplace comfy.

2. Imagine all the bad thoughts — the memories of your day, the negative feelings — as a yucky-coloured liquid.

3. Let that liquid flow out of your body through your fingers and toes. Feel your body emptying. See it in your mind's eye, draining out and away.

4. When all the muck is gone, picture a pleasant colour of your choice — a warm, sunshiny gold, a soothing blue. Now imagine it pouring into the top of your head and filling you up with its glorious light. As your body fills with light, think about how it makes you feel peaceful.

Control Your Breath

Controlling your breath is one of the most powerful stress-reducers on the planet. It doesn't happen automatically though. The more you practise, the better you get at it — and the easier it will be when you need to feel calmer.

Try this breathing exercise to get even more peace-power:

1. Breathe in for a count of four.
2. Hold your breath for a count of two.
3. Let the breath out slowly, for a count of eight.
4. Repeat six to twelve times.

Keep Breathing

This breathing technique is said to be cooling to the mind and spirit. It's fun too!

1. Sit comfortably on the floor or a chair, keeping your back straight.

2. Lower your chin a bit. Stick out your tongue and roll it, if you can, into the shape of a hot dog bun.

3. With your tongue still sticking out, breathe in through your mouth, slowly lifting your chin toward the ceiling. Can you feel the coolness of the air flowing over your tongue?

4. When you're ready to exhale, pull in your tongue and close your mouth. Breathe out through your nose as you lower your chin to a level position.

5. Repeat eight to twelve times.

Take Time for a Pick-Me-Up

You can consciously control your breath to help you feel calmer. But sometimes, like right before a test, you want to feel relaxed and alert. Try this technique for a pick-me-up:

1. Hold your right thumb over your right nostril.
2. Breathe in deeply through your left nostril.
3. When you're ready to exhale, let go of your right thumb and pinch the left nostril closed with your ring finger.
4. Breathe out through the right nostril.
5. Repeat steps 1 to 4, eight to twelve times.

Give Yourself a Pep Talk

Does that little voice in your head give you a hard time sometimes? You know the one — it says, "You're going to blow this." That's called negative self-talk.

Give yourself a pep talk instead. Tell yourself, "I prepared for this. I know my stuff and I practised tons! I've got it down, and I'm going to rock!"

Your brain believes whatever you tell it. So make sure you tell it the truth — that you are bound to succeed.

Here are some more ways to pump yourself up:

Negative Self-Talk: I'm going to blow it — I've never done this before.
Pep Talk: This is a great chance to learn something new, and I love learning new things.

Negative Self-Talk: It's too hard.
Pep Talk: A little hard work won't kill me! I'll break it down into chunks and gradually get the hang of it.

Negative Self-Talk: I don't know how to do it.
Pep Talk: I can learn anything I set my mind to. I'm smart and capable.

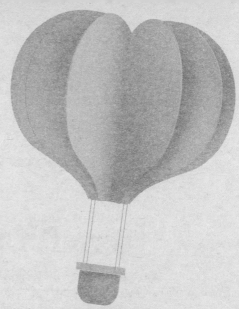

Negative Self-Talk: I've always been terrible at that.
Pep Talk: I never really tried my best before. I can practise and get better. I've got plenty of grit and determination.

Negative Self-Talk: There's no way it will work.
Pep Talk: I can try to make it work. I've got a fighter's spirit!

Negative Self-Talk: It's too risky.
Pep Talk: I'm a brave person. And really, what have I got to lose?

Negative Self-Talk: No one likes me.
Pep Talk: I'm very likeable.

Negative Self-Talk: I've tried and I can't do it.
Pep Talk: I'll give it another try. And if that still doesn't work, I'll ask for help. Where there's a will, there's a way, and I've got plenty of will!

Turn Off the Filter

You just got home from your best friend's
birthday party. When you think about the party,
what do you remember: the compliments you got
on your outfit, how people laughed at your joke
about the elephant, or how that kid you barely
know helped you clean up when you spilled
the pop? Or do you recall the moment you
discovered you had parsley in your teeth, no one
laughed at your clown joke, and you drenched
the rug in cola?

Filtering out the good things and focusing on
the negatives is a sneakily destructive habit. It
saps your self-esteem and robs you of happy
memories. It makes you feel more stressed and
anxious.

The next time you find yourself focusing on
something bad that happened, make an active
effort to recall something positive *that also
happened.* You'll wind up with a more realistic
view of the world and yourself.

It's Not about You

You walk down the hallway at school and notice clusters of kids giggling together. Do you automatically think they must be laughing at you?

Or a group of friends suddenly cancels plans. Do you assume It's because they don't want to hang with you anymore?

If this sounds like you, you may be prone to a mental glitch called *personalization*. It means you tend to think you are somehow the cause of whatever's happening around you.

The truth is, the only person who is spending tons of time thinking about you is you. Everyone else is up to the eyeballs thinking about — you guessed it — themselves.

So chances are the kids in the hall aren't laughing at you, but at something funny someone just said. And plans get cancelled all the time, for lots of reasons. Most of them have nothing to do with you.

If you find yourself slipping into the personalization trap, give your head a shake and think of two or three more likely explanations for what just happened. One of them is probably the truth.

You're not the centre of the universe after all. Isn't that a relief?

Go Grey

Do you tend to see the world in black or white?

Black-and-white thinkers have very clear divisions in their minds about what's right or wrong, good or bad, perfection or failure. There's no in-between. Their mental categories tend to be quite rigid too.

This kind of thinking can cause you lots of stress because, as it turns out, the world isn't strictly black and white. For example, some might say mosquitoes are annoying pests. But they also provide a much-needed food source for birds and fish. Without mosquitoes, many other animals would die.

People who see the world in many shades of grey get a more realistic picture of how things are. They understand that a mosquito can be bad in one circumstance but good in another.

When you start seeing the world in shades of grey, a whole new world opens up for you.

Get Going

It doesn't seem like worrying is a pleasant way to spend your time. But from your brain's point of view, worrying feels good.

The act of worrying actually triggers the brain's pleasure centres. That's because it feels like you're doing something. Worrying about the future feels productive, even when it isn't.

Whenever you feel yourself getting caught in the worry trap, try this:

1. Jot down a description of what you are worrying about.

2. Then make a list of ways to prevent, reduce or avoid it.

3. Now that you've done something that's actually useful, you can stop worrying!

4. Still feeling tense? Take a walk or get some other exercise to give your brain and body something else to do.

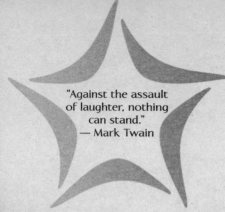

Giggle

Giggle. Guffaw. Chuckle. Chortle. Hee-haw. A good laugh is the greatest stress-buster out there.

So watch a funny video, make a goofy face at a friend or share some terrible, terrible jokes around the dinner table.

Laughter really is the best medicine.

People Watch

On the bus, in the lunchroom, at the park — wherever there are people, there's endless opportunity for people-watching.

Focus on that pair who are deep in conversation. Who are they? Friends? Sisters? And what are they talking about?

Check out that child wailing at the top of his lungs. What set him off?

Imagining stories about strangers is a great way to pass the time. And it keeps you from mulling over the everyday worries that might otherwise fill up your brain.

It's also a super way to help you learn to read body language — a skill that can help you get along better with others.

Take a Mindful Walk

Getting outdoors and going for a walk is a time-honoured way of reducing stress. To get even *more* stress relief from your ramble, make it a mindful walk.

Pay close attention to your footsteps. How do your feet feel when they hit the pavement? Can you hear the sound? Is your footfall a steady rhythm? Quick or slow?

As you walk, make note of what you see. What do you smell? How does the sun or wind or rain feel on your cheeks?

Focus on the sensation of your body as it moves through space. Do your arms swing by your sides, or are your hands tucked into your pockets. Do your hips sway? Can you hear your own breath? Are you smiling or is there a furrow in your brow?

When you walk mindfully, you clear your mind of clutter. You can see the world, and your place in it, more clearly too.

Label It!

Your day is full of many experiences and so many emotions, it can sometimes feel confusing and overwhelming. One way to get a handle on all those swirling feelings is to name them.

Here's how:

1. When a strong emotion washes over you, don't try to push it away. Recognize and acknowledge it.
2. Ask yourself what word best describes the emotion you are feeling.
3. Accept the feeling.

This simple process helps lessen negative feelings and gives you a chance to control them and your behaviour in more positive ways. You'll be less likely to snap at your dad when he asks you to set the table, or fly into a rage when you misplace your hairbrush.

Labelling your feelings will also help you to share them with others. If a friend upsets you, you'll be able to explain how you feel and patch things up.

Show Your Hands Some Love

Your hands work hard for you all day. They also carry a lot of tension.

Show your hands some love with a mini-massage. You can do it anywhere, anytime!

1. Use a moisturizer. Choose one with a pleasant or relaxing scent, like lavender.

2. Beginning at the base of your left pinkie, gently massage each joint and each section of each finger.

3. Now massage the palm, paying special attention to the pad at the base of your thumb.

4. Stretch your fingers as wide as you can for a few seconds, then relax them.

5. Make as tight a fist as you can for a few seconds, then let it go.

6. Rotate your wrist a few times in each direction.

7. Gently squeeze and roll the skin between your thumb and forefinger.

8. Repeat on your right hand.

Get In Touch

Maybe you're not the huggy type, but research shows that people who have more physical contact with others tend to be happier and more relaxed.

Here are some fun ways to get in touch:

- Take someone for a piggyback ride.
- Have a thumb-wrestling contest.
- Engage in some playful roughhousing with your buds.
- Play touch football.
- Play a hand-clapping game.
- Draw letters on a friend's back and have them guess what you're spelling out.
- Play Hot Hands — the game where you put your hands on top of the other person's and they try and slap them before you take them away.
- Crack an imaginary egg on your friend's head, and let your fingers mimic the egg dripping down their back.

Watch the Clock

Try this simple breathing activity for five minutes to help you relax. You will need a watch or clock with a second hand, or a stopwatch.

- Breathing normally, count how many times you inhale and exhale in one minute — count one inhale and one exhale as one.

- Keep watching the clock for the second and third minutes. Does your breathing slow down?

- Consciously try to slow your breathing.

Aw, Baby

This yoga pose, called "Baby Pose," is a fast and easy stress reliever.

1. Lie on your back with your feet in the air.
2. Bring your knees to your chest. Grab the outside of both feet.
3. Gently rock from side to side and up and down, giving your back a light massage.
4. Then let your legs flop back to the ground and all of your muscles relax.

Ditch the Junk Food

Like a car or an airplane, your body requires high-quality fuel to function at its best. Junk foods — highly processed foods that are low in nutrients and high in sugars and fats — are sneaky. They make you feel full, but they keep your energy tanks empty. No wonder you feel out of gas.

Eating more healthy foods — fresh fruits and vegetables that offer a good balance of protein, fat and carbohydrates — and fewer processed foods will keep your energy tanks full. It will also help keep your mood on a more even keel, so you feel fewer sharp ups and downs. You'll be able to handle the stresses in your life more gracefully.

Make Some Soup

There's nothing like soup to make you feel
warm all over. It soothes the soul after a trying
day, and a nutritious meal also helps refill your
energy tanks.

It's super easy to make too. Open up a can
of your favourite soup; pour hot water over
ramen noodles; or toss some odds and ends
from the fridge into a pot, add water and some
seasonings and treat yourself to a spoonful of
heaven.

Take Yourself Less Seriously

So you came out of the washroom with toilet paper stuck to your shoe. It's really not a calamity — it's cause for hilarity.

And that bad case of bedhead? Big deal. It happens to everyone.

Go ahead — laugh at yourself. You're pretty funny, after all.

Trace in Space

Need a minibreak? Look around you for an interesting pattern, such as in a carpet or the wallpaper. Choose one line and follow it with your eyes. Then follow it back or in another direction.

Is there a design on the cover of your notebook or in the tabletop? Trace it with your finger. Close your eyes and let your finger follow the same path back.

Do a Craft

Cut, fold, paste. Knit, purl, knit. Hammer, saw, clamp.

Making something yourself is super satisfying. It can be a painting or a canoe. It can be built with old buttons or electronic doodads.

As you become immersed in your project, you'll feel time slipping away — you'll enter "the zone," where people feel happiest and most satisfied. You'll forget about your worries.

And when you're done, even if your creation is lumpy or lopsided, sit back and bask in a well-earned sense of accomplishment. You made it!

Celebrate Boredom

A recent study confirmed that many people would prefer receiving a series of electric shocks than enduring ten minutes of boredom.

While boredom can be painful, it also serves a purpose. When there's no external stimulation, it forces you to turn inward to your own thoughts and feelings.

From moments like these comes greater self-awareness. You might be forced to deal with problems you've been avoiding. You might even find that the quiet period gives you a much-needed moment of peace in a too-hurried day.

So if boredom strikes, don't fight it. Accept it and wait to see what unexpected gifts it brings.

Is Your Head in the Clouds?

Maybe it should be.

Look up — *waaaay* up. What do you see up there in the sky? Do you see a fluffy, white cloud or a camel? A wisp of cumulonimbus or a dog bone?

Nature is asking to play with you. Won't you join in?

Let Your Mind Drift

A little daydreaming is good for the soul.

Let your mind drift.

Stare out the window.

Doodle in your notebook.

Indulge in a pleasant fantasy (You're a superhero! A rock star!) or two.

A few minutes of zoning out can actually be good for you. It refreshes your brain so you can focus better when you return. It helps your imagination go to work to solve pesky problems. If you daydream about achieving a goal, it can even motivate you to work harder to make it come true.

Make a Labyrinth

Since medieval times, monks and religious pilgrims have used labyrinths — curving paths that lead to a central point, then back out again — as an aid to meditation and contemplation.

Today many people still find walking through a labyrinth is a wonderful tool for clearing their minds and relieving stress.

You don't need anything fancy to create a labyrinth for yourself — just a plot of concrete and a piece of chalk, or a field of snow and your own footprints. Trace out a design like the one on this page, large enough so you can walk on it.

Then, take a moment to centre yourself and slowly walk along the path, deep into the heart of your maze, and back out again.

Dealing with Those Awkward Moments

Everyone feels shy sometimes. Try these tips for turning awkward moments into *aha!* ones.

- Ask other people questions. This takes your mind off you and your nerves. Then listen carefully to the answer.

- Switch off your imagination. Stop wondering about what other people are thinking and spinning your own interpretations. Focus instead on what people are doing — and join in!

- Take careful note of your surroundings. What does the room look like? What colours are people wearing? Shifting your focus to external details like these helps you to relax and enjoy yourself.

- Be yourself. If you're sometimes goofy and sometimes say the wrong thing, that's okay. When you're true to yourself, people will want to be around you!

Set Reasonable Limits

There are so many fun things to do — skating practice, learning to juggle, reading — and so many obligations too — homework, household chores, babysitting. It's easy to take on too much.

Know what your limits are. Do you need nine hours of sleep to feel rested? Then make sure you get it. Do you need at least an hour of chill time every day after school? Then keep that precious time free.

It might mean occasionally saying no to something you want to do, but you'll feel happier and more able to enjoy the activities you say yes to in the end.

Say Thank You

There are so many people who do things for you every day — teachers, caregivers, friends, even strangers who hold open the door or give you a seat on the bus.

Make sure to say "thank you" to all of them! They'll get a lift and so will you.

It's Not Personal

You were hanging out with your best pal when all of a sudden, *SNAP!* He lashed out at you. You have no idea what you did to set him off. Maybe you did nothing at all.

Sometimes other people have the same issues you do. They're short of sleep or hungry. They can't find the right words for a feeling. They've had enough.

Give your pal some space.

You'll find out soon enough if this outburst was a one-time thing or something bigger.

Under Pressure

Pressing down on specific points on your feet or wrists is said to help with stress relief. Press on the points described below for two to three minutes each. Make sure to pay attention to your breathing, keeping it slow and steady, to get the best results.

Wrists: Hold your hand, palm up. Press on the pinky side of your wrist just below where your wrist bends.

Feet: Press on the sole of your foot about a quarter of the way down from the third toe.

Ear This

You know how much dogs love to have their ears rubbed? It's a great stress reliever for humans too!

Gently grip each of your earlobes between a thumb and forefinger. Rub them this way and that for as long as three minutes.

Don't be surprised if you feel ready for a follow-up belly rub.

Shake It!

Qigong is an ancient health and relaxation practice that includes elements from Chinese medicine and martial arts.

To help relax, qigong practitioners shake their bodies for two to three minutes. It's easy, it's fun and it works.

Give this qigong exercise a try:

1. Stand in a relaxed posture with your arms by your sides.
2. Bend your knees a bit and start bouncing up and down.
3. With your arms relaxed, start to shake them. Shake, shake, shake!
4. When you've finished, your entire body will feel warm and loose.

Touch the Sky

Can you touch the sky? Try it and see.

1. Raise your hands over your head, as high as you can.
2. Stretch even higher.
3. Raise up on your tippytoes to take you even higher.
4. STRETCH!
5. Doesn't that feel . . . *aaah?*

Stargaze

On a clear night, head outdoors and look up at the sky. Can you see stars?

Think about how far away they are — millions of kilometres. Think about how huge they are and how tiny you are by comparison. As you consider these other suns and galaxies, let the grandeur of the universe wash over you. Your own problems may suddenly seem much smaller.

Ragdoll

After a stretch or a hard day, it's great to let it all go.

From a standing position, bend at the waist, letting your head and arms hang down. Feel gravity take over — let your head and arms go heavy and limp. Sway gently from side to side. Let your knees soften.

When you've finished, stand up slowly, rolling up one vertebra at a time, and bringing your head up last.

Cuddle

Curl up with Fluffy. Grab a teddy bear. Lean your head on your dad's shoulder.

Giving and getting a cuddle from someone special is a surefire way to warm your heart and sweeten your day.

Have a Ball!

Dribble it. Kick it. Spike it.

Bunt it. Shoot it into the corner pocket. Pass it. Put a spin on it.

Roll it, bowl it, bump it, dump it, whack it, smack it.

Getting active is a top way to blow off steam and reduce stress. It's also a ton of fun.

So grab a ball and you're guaranteed to have one.

Check Out a Map

Feeling lost or like you've gotten off track? Consider that there's more than one route to success.

Pick up a map, any map. Take a look at all the roadways on it.

There are many ways to get from *here* to *there*. Some are crowded. Some wind through pretty but tough terrain. Some go to nearby familiar places. Some take you to faraway lands. Some can only be travelled single file. Some are straight and fast with few exits. Some have tolls.

All of them are there waiting for you to decide your own unique itinerary.

Be Like a Tree

When you feel like your life is off-balance, try this re-centring yoga pose called "Tree Pose." It will help quiet your mind as it strengthens your body.

1. Stand comfortably, gazing straight ahead. Lower your shoulders away from your ears and draw your shoulder blades together to open your chest.

2. Place your hands on your hips.

3. Bend the right knee and point it to the wall to your right. Rest the sole of your foot against your left leg.

4. Slowly slide the right foot up the inside of the left leg until it rests on the calf or thigh (not the knee).

5. Press down all the corners of the left foot on the floor while you press in with the right foot. Draw up your kneecap on your left leg to help stabilize you.

6. Hold as long as you can, then switch feet and repeat.

Find the Balance

It takes work to create balance in your life. While you practise Tree Pose, consider where you are putting your energy in your daily life. Are you spending too much time studying and not enough time socializing? Or the reverse?

Aim for a healthy balance between time spent on work, relationships and looking after your physical health.

It's tough to get the mix exactly right — and it won't stay right forever! Just like when you practise tree pose, you may find yourself wobbling. Take a deep breath and make adjustments. You'll get it!

Make Today a Holiday

Hooray! It's . . . Tuesday?

Turn any day into a holiday with a burst of imagination. Say it's Celebrate Sock Day and make a banner for your wall featuring striped kneehighs. Bake cupcakes decorated with pics of polka dot socks. Don a stocking cap.

Or call it National Pineapple Day and dress all in yellow.

Backwards Day . . .

Funny Face Day . . .

Tell a Bad Joke Day . . .

The possibilities are endless.

If you have trouble fitting in a longer workout, aim for ten minutes at a time, four or five times a day.

Pump It Up

Your body is made to move. When you've been sitting all day, you're bound to get tense and cranky.

So get moving! Do any activity that gets your heart pumping and your skin sweaty.

Aerobic exercise helps get rid of excess cortisol, the hormone associated with stress. It also stimulates the release of endorphins, the hormones that make you feel good. Try dancing, running up and down the stairs, practising your juggling moves — anything that gets you off your duff and moving.

Krazy Karaoke

Crank up the tunes, feel the beat and belt out a song.

Sing along to your favourite songs in your room. No one else has to know. Or get a gang together for a karaoke party. You're bound to have a laugh while you burn off excess energy.

Go Out and Play

Feel the wind on your cheeks, the ground under your running shoes and joy in your heart. Nature is the best stress-reliever in the world.

Play an old-fashioned game like Red Rover, Spud or Capture the Flag.

Make daisy chains, snow angels or autumn leaf bouquets.

Draw with sidewalk chalk or paint a fence with coloured water.

Or simply observe the natural world around you.

It doesn't matter what you do, as long as you get outside so nature can work its magic on you.

Try a Soothing Nature App

If you've got a smart phone, you know what a distraction it can be. Checking it over and over again for new messages or scrolling endlessly through a social media feed not only takes time but can up your stress level. Reliance on your phone can become a bad habit very quickly and rob you of other experiences that are more pleasurable or valuable in the long run.

The trick is to use your phone wisely. Turn off notifications that constantly clamour for your attention. And turn off your phone altogether during times you don't want any distractions — like when you're in class or with friends or family.

Consider loading apps that will help you reduce stress. These can include . . .

- meditation apps that give you 5 or 10 minutes of guidance in basic meditation techniques.
- nature apps that let you listen to soothing sounds of birdsong, waves crashing on a beach or wind through pines.
- music designed for relaxation.

Mother Nature's Got Your Back

We usually think of gravity as the force that makes objects fall to the ground. But there's another way to think about it — it's also the force of Mother Earth pulling you toward her heart.

Lie down on your back and close your eyes. Can you feel how the Earth is actually supporting you?

When you feel like things are too much to handle on your own, remember that Mother Earth has always got your back.

Cook or Bake Something

Food nourishes the body, but it also nourishes the soul. Preparing food — for yourself and for others — makes you feel good. You feel proud of your accomplishment and bask in the praise from the folks who taste what you've made. Best of all, you get to make what you like to eat!

What should you make? Try . . .

- a no-cook yogurt dip to serve with cut-up fresh veggies
- a fresh salad chock full of juicy tomatoes, crisp cucumbers and crunchy pumpkin seeds with homemade mustard vinaigrette
- cheese-sprinkled or garlic-salted popcorn
- mile-high club sandwiches
- a microwave chocolate cake in a cup
- oatmeal cookies
- an easy to make quick bread like corn, zucchini or banana bread

Just Be

Sometimes we equate what we do (gymnastics, math) with who we are. But you are you, no matter what you do. And that alone is enough — enough to deserve respect, to be considered worthwhile, to claim your space on this planet.

So take a few moments to just quietly enjoy being in your own skin, being here now and experiencing the wonder and the magic of being alive.

Celebrate yourself.

Skip the Comparisons

Do you tend to compare yourself to others? If you do, you will frequently find yourself coming up short.

Life isn't fair. Not everyone starts in the same place, with the same gifts or strengths. That's why you can only judge yourself against yourself. Otherwise you're comparing apples to oranges.

Instead of using others as a measuring stick, use your own goals and your own progress to chart your success. And take pride in your achievements, no matter how small. Why? Because you've earned them.

Be Kind to Future You

You know you have to clean up your room, but you are happily involved in a video game. So you say to yourself, "I'll do it after dinner." Somehow you think Future You will be happier about doing that chore than Now You.

But then dinner is done and you're ready to flop. Future You is now Now You — and Now You still doesn't want to clean your room. In fact, you wish you'd done it earlier, when you weren't yawning like mad and eager for bed.

When you procrastinate, you guarantee aggravation for Future You.

So be kind to Future You. If you've got the ability to accomplish something now, do it! Future You will be *soooo* grateful.

Enjoy the Journey

Having goals is great, but life is a journey.

Don't forget to stop and smell the flowers along the way.

Keep your eye on the prize, but enjoy each and every day.

Read Fiction

Feel like taking a break from the real world for a while? Reading is a great escape, and reading fiction is the best escape of all. Not only will you travel to new places, you'll meet new people and find out what it's like to be inside their skin and see the world through their eyes.

Reading novels, graphic novels, short stories and fan fiction is also great for helping build empathy. Kids who read more fiction wind up with a better understanding of how other people feel than those who don't. They grow more caring and less judgmental. That skill helps you get along better with others.

Reading fiction helps you read people.

Create a Vision Board

Have you got a goal that you're working toward? Or a dream that gives you pleasure to think about? Put it on a vision board. Use a simple bulletin board, piece of bristol board or cardboard to tack up pictures, quotes, photos — anything that pertains to your idea and helps you see it more clearly.

You can also make a vision board to help you keep track of the steps you need to complete a task or inspire you to stay on course. For example, if you hate tidying your room, a vision board of attractive, tidy, relaxing spaces can help motivate you to toss those jammies in the hamper.

Enjoy the Sound of Silence

Airplanes whiz overhead. Sirens blare down the street. Voices, voices, voices — noise is everywhere! Noise can even be considered a form of pollution.

If your nerves feel jangled, try taking a silent retreat. Find a quiet place where you can tune everything out — the corner of the school library or in your own bathtub. Put on headphones or stuff your ears with cotton. Whether it's for a few minutes or a few days, a period of total silence can be soothing to the mind, soul and body.

Enjoy the sound of silence, and let it bring you peace.

Do a Repetitive Task

Rake the leaves. Fold laundry. Dry dishes.

None of these chores sounds like a barrel of laughs, but they bring their own pleasure.

Repetitive motions soothe the central nervous system. They make you feel calmer. At the same time, seeing that pile of leaves grow or the dishes gleam in the rack gives you a sense of achievement.

So when you need a break, do some work.

It really works!

Get Rid of Pesky Irritations

Is the tag on the inside of your shirt scratching the back of your neck? Cut it off.

Is your pen leaking? Get a new one.

Is there an annoying hole in the fingertip of your wool glove? Sew it up.

Small irritations can get under your skin. They interfere with your concentration, making you tire faster. They chip away at your ability to handle bigger and more important stresses, like that nerve-wracking science test.

Make a Don't-Do List

You probably have a "To-Do" list to help keep you on track. But what about a "Don't-Do" list?

Consider the distracting or negative habits that sometimes get in your way, like gossiping, or filling up on chips before dinner. Put them on your "Don't-Do" list as a handy reminder.

A quick scan of your list might help keep you focused on what you *should do* — and help you avoid unnecessary stress.

Get Some Sleep

You're so worked up, you can't fall asleep. And now you've got another worry — that you'll be too tired tomorrow to handle the challenges coming your way.

Try these tips to help you deal.

- Jot down a brief description of what's worrying you and set it aside. Tell yourself you'll deal with it in the morning. In doing so, you give yourself permission to get to sleep.

- Try not to look at the clock. It will only make you feel more stressed and less able to sleep.

- Don't worry about not sleeping! Everybody has occasional sleepless nights. For most people, one bad night doesn't make much difference in how you function the next day.

Take a nap. A twenty-minute daytime nap is equal to a full hour of sleep at night.

Better than Sheep

When the eyes-wide-open-at-midnight monster takes hold of your mind, don't just take it lying down! Get up. Letting the same thoughts spin around and around while you try to ignore them simply doesn't work. Instead get out of bed and engage in a simple, soothing activity. It acts like a reset button for your brain, so you can get back to sleep.

Choose a reset activity that is diverting, but not too absorbing. So skip brain-busting puzzles or that page-turner graphic novel. Avoid looking for long at a screen too; the bluish light that most phones and computers give off affects levels of melatonin (the hormone that makes you feel sleepy) in your brain. That makes it harder to get back to sleep. Try these super reset ideas:

- Walk around a bit.
- Drink a small glass of water.
- Brush your hair.
- Lay out your clothes for the next morning.
- Do some relaxing yoga poses or stretches.
- Turn on a soft light and read a book.
- Listen to some relaxing music.
- Colour or draw for a few minutes.

Sunrise, Sunset

If you're an early riser, you can start your day with some quiet time watching the sunrise. Enjoy the colours. Contemplate how every day brings its own unique beauty.

Then when evening comes, take a few minutes to watch the sunset. Use the opportunity to let the stress of the day melt away along with the colours of the sky.